FOOD and FARMING

From FARM *to* TABLE

Richard and Louise Spilsbury

PowerKiDS
press.
New York

Published in 2011 by The Rosen Publishing Group Inc.
29 East 21st Street, New York, NY 10010

First Edition

Editor: Julia Adams
Managing Editor, Discovery Books: Rachel Tisdale
Editor, Discovery Books: Jenny Vaughan
Designer and Illustrator: Graham Rich
Picture Researcher: Bobby Humphrey
Consultant: Nicholas Rowles

Library of Congress Cataloging-in-Publication Data

Spilsbury, Richard, 1963-
  From farm to table / by Richard and Louise Spilsbury. — 1st ed.
    p. cm. — (Food and farming)
  Includes index.
  ISBN 978-1-61532-580-1 (library binding)
  ISBN 978-1-61532-589-4 (paperback)
  ISBN 978-1-61532-590-0 (6-pack)
  1. Food industry and trade—Juvenile literature. 2. Food supply—Juvenile literature.
  I. Spilsbury, Louise. II. Title. III. Series: Food and farming.
  TP370.3.S65 2011
  664—dc22

                              2009045756

Photographs:
Alamy: p. 15 (Tengku Mohd Yusof); CFW Images: p. 14 (Chris Fairclough);
Fletchersalads.co.uk/ www.usedhorticulturalmachinery.com: p. 7; Getty Images: pp. 6 (Prakash
Singh/AFP), 11 (Klaus P. Exner), 10 (Alberto Incrocci), 12 (Justin Lightley), 27 (Niurka
Barroso/AFP), 29 (Adrian Weinbrecht), cover top (Dave Reede); Bobby Humphrey: p. 25;
Istockphoto.com: pp. 4, cover bottom, 9 & 23 (Jason Alan), 20 (Jo Gough), 21 (Jillian Pond),
24 (Sean Locke), 28 (Vasiliki Varvaki); Shutterstock: pp. 5 (iofoto), 13 (Mark Yuill), 17
(Shutterlist), 18 & title page (Elena Aliaga), 19 (Eduardo Rivero), 23

Manufactured in China
CPSIA Compliance Information: Batch #WAS0102PK: For Further Information
contact Rosen Publishing, New York, New York at 1-800-237-9932

CONTENTS

PRODUCING FOOD

Food is mostly produced on farms. There are many types and sizes of farms all over the world, growing and producing many different kinds of food.

Subsistence and Commercial Farms

In poor countries, many farmers have small areas of land, where they grow food for themselves and their families. If there is any surplus, it is sold in local markets. Food here travels only a short distance from the farms to people's tables. Commercial farms grow large amounts of crops and other foods for sale. Some are arable farms, which grow crops such as grains or vegetables. Livestock or pastoral farms keep animals, usually for meat but sometimes for milk, too. Mixed farms raise both animals and crops. Many of these farms grow several kinds of crops, such as different types of fruit and vegetables, as well as rearing

◀ *On subsistence farms, such as this one in Thailand, the farmer's family eats food that is grown only a few steps from their home.*

▲ *The food in your shopping cart may come from farms in many different states or countries, all around the world.*

animals. Others produce just one kind of food. For example, orchards may grow only apples and dairy farms may only have cows to produce milk for dairy products.

The Food Industry

Commercial farms are part of a global industry that employs over 16 million workers. After crops, livestock, and other foods have been grown and harvested, they are cleaned, sorted, and often, processed into food products. Food is transported and distributed all over the world. Sales of processed foods add up to over $1.65 trillion worldwide. Huge amounts of money are needed to pay for wages, farm equipment, and chemicals, and for the other resources, such as water and electricity, used in the business of food production and distribution.

CONSUMPTION

An adult body needs enough food to supply about 2,500 calories of energy per day. However, the amount people actually eat depends more on how much money they have than how much energy they need. For instance, people in rich countries in Europe often eat as much as 1.5 times the number of calories they need. In poor countries, such as Rwanda or Afghanistan, people eat only 0.75 times the number of calories their bodies need.

GLOBAL CROPS

Today, crops and animals that are produced on a farm in one country often end up in another, far away. The increasing trade in food across the world is part of a system of trading between countries called globalization.

Food Seasons

In many parts of the world, growing conditions vary at different seasons of the year. For example, locally grown beans are ready for sale only in the summer in northern Europe. At any other time of year, the only beans available have been grown many thousands of miles away, for instance, in Kenya. Globalization allows consumers to eat foods independently of the seasons and the climate where they live. Beans can be imported into northern countries, when they cannot be grown at home. Some crops always have to be imported, since they can only grow in certain climates. Mangoes, which grow in the tropics, are an example of this.

◄ *In India, mangoes are at their best in late spring. At that time of the year, large numbers can be exported to countries where mangoes do not naturally grow.*

Availability and Cost

Globalization also means that countries with not enough farmland than they need to feed their populations can import food. For example, Japan imports 70 percent of the grain it uses. Globalization makes it possible for companies to buy food cheaply from farmers in poor parts of the world, where wages are low, and make money by selling it at a higher price to consumers in rich countries. Commercial farmers all over the world depend on consumers to buy their food, and the consumers depend on farmers to provide it: the farmers and the consumers of the food they produce are interdependent.

▲ *Some crops, such as squash, grow in an irregular way all over the plant, and it is impossible to pick them by machine. They have to be harvested by hand.*

HAND HARVEST

Machines are more widely used by farmers in rich countries than in poor ones but, all over the world, many crops are harvested by hand because machines can damage them. In the United States, about 25 percent of vegetables and 45 percent of fruit are hand harvested. At harvest time, extra jobs are often created on farms because crops need to be picked when they are ripe.

FOOD FROM GRAINS

Grains, such as wheat, rice, and corn, grow on more of the world's farmland than any other crops. They are members of the grass family, and farmers grow them for their tough, carbohydrate-filled seeds.

Rice

Grain carbohydrates supply the majority of food energy for billions of people worldwide. They are among the most important staple foods (main energy-giving foods in a community). Rice is the staple food for more than half the world's population. Many people who depend on it live in poor countries in Asia. Farmers harvest the grains from rice plants and remove the inedible husks around

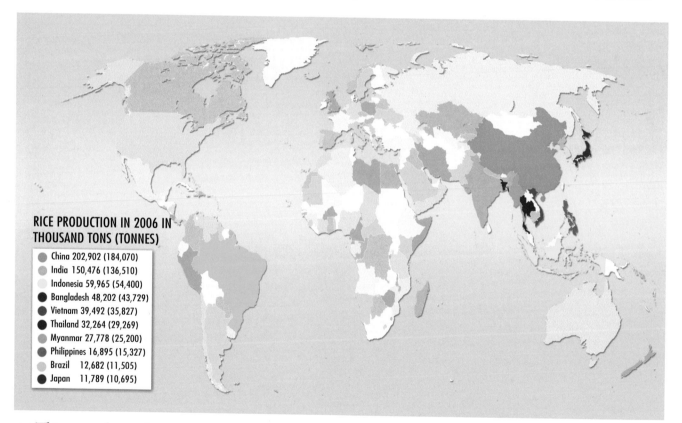

RICE PRODUCTION IN 2006 IN THOUSAND TONS (TONNES)

- China 202,902 (184,070)
- India 150,476 (136,510)
- Indonesia 59,965 (54,400)
- Bangladesh 48,202 (43,729)
- Vietnam 39,492 (35,827)
- Thailand 32,264 (29,269)
- Myanmar 27,778 (25,200)
- Philippines 16,895 (15,327)
- Brazil 12,682 (11,505)
- Japan 11,789 (10,695)

▲ *This map shows the main rice-growing areas of the world. Rice grows best in warm, wet climates, especially in south and southeastern Asia. China and India are the biggest producers. China's crop is over 198 million tons (180 million t) a year; India's is nearly 154 million tons (140 million t).*

the seeds, which leaves brown rice. This can be done by machine. Over two-thirds of brown rice is then processed to remove the rice bran, to create white rice. People prefer to buy white rice for its appearance, softness, and ease of cooking. However, without nutrients from rice bran, which aids digestion, white rice is less healthy to eat than brown rice.

Wheat Flour

After harvesting, most wheat grains are ground into flour, usually by using machines powered by electricity. These crush the grains between steel rollers or stone disks. The flour is used to make foods such as breads and pasta. These are made by mixing flour with water, oil, and other ingredients to make dough. Most pasta is made in factories, where the dough is shaped and dried before sale. Bakers make bread dough into loaves or rolls, which they bake to be eaten fresh.

▲ *Eating bread made from flour is one of most common ways of using wheat. People have been baking different kinds of bread for around 10,000 years.*

BREAD

People worldwide use flour from wheat grains to make bread, which is a staple food. Often, they add yeast to the bread dough. Yeast is made up of tiny organisms that release carbon dioxide gas as they consume sugar in warm water. Bubbles of the gas make the dough expand and rise.

Fruit and vegetable crops are processed in many different ways on their journey from the farm to the table. This processing begins on the farm, long before the produce reaches the world's stores.

On the Farm

The first part of processing is when farm workers wash soil off any harvested vegetables. They trim tattered or discolored leaves from the outside of lettuces and cauliflowers and remove impurities, such as pieces of stone or dead insects picked up during harvesting. Farmers also sort crops before they leave the farm. On commercial farms, they often use machines that automatically (and rapidly) measure the fruit, because some supermarket chains only buy fruit above a certain size, or pay more for larger crops. Fruit and vegetables must also be sorted for quality. For example, holes in the skin of an apple might be a sign of an insect inside the fruit. Some farms have X-ray machines that can view inside their produce, to make checking easier.

▶ *A factory worker inspects a crop of beans to make sure they are of good enough quality to sell in supermarkets.*

DEBATE

Is Meat Production a Good Use of Resources?

Millions of people are vegetarians, who never eat meat. Some go further, and are vegans, who eat nothing produced by living animals, such as milk, eggs, or even honey. People may become vegetarians or vegans because they believe it is wrong to kill animals. Others choose not to eat animal products because they believe that these waste the world's resources. For instance, it takes about two pounds of grain to produce one pound of chicken and seven to produce a pound of beef. This can be seen as an inefficient use of land.

Juices and Oils

Some harvested plants are made into juices or oils, usually at a factory called a processing plant. The most common juice produced globally is orange juice. Ripe oranges are pressed in powerful machines and the juice is collected. Sometimes, the juice is heated so water evaporates, leaving concentrated juice that takes up less space and is lighter to transport. The two countries where most oranges grow are Brazil and the United States. Plantations (very large farms) in these countries produce enough juice each year to fill 100 of the biggest supertankers. Other common juices include apple, pineapple, and grape. Cooking and salad oils are produced by pressing olives or seeds and nuts, such as sunflower seeds and peanuts.

▶ *For centuries, people have pressed olives to extract their oil, which is used in salad dressings and for cooking.*

IN THE DAIRY

Dairy farms produce milk. Milk is a mixture of fat or cream, nutrients including protein, a kind of sugar called lactose, the mineral calcium, and water.

Processing Milk

Much of the dairy farming in rich countries is practiced on a large scale by commercial farmers. Cows are milked by machine. This raw milk may contain harmful bacteria, so when it is taken from the farm to the dairy, it is pasteurized. This involves heating milk rapidly to destroy the bacteria. The pasteurized milk is then moved through chilled pipes into cool tanks to keep it fresh. Dairies may process milk further, to remove some or all of the fat in it, or to dry it out to make milk powder. Milk can also be processed and changed to make dairy products, such as yogurt, cheese, and butter.

◀ *A cheesemaker checks a traditionally-produced cheese to see if it is ripe and of a good quality.*

▲ *Yogurt is often produced on a large scale and packed mechanically, ready for sale.*

Yogurt and Cheese

Farmers or dairies make yogurt by adding special bacteria to warmed milk. The bacteria change the lactose in the milk into a sour substance called lactic acid. This gives yogurt its sharp flavor and makes it thick. Farmers or dairies make most cheeses by adding acid and rennet to warm milk. Rennet is a substance that makes the milk separate into solid lumps called curds and watery liquid called whey. Cheesemakers drain off the whey and add salt to the curds, which they press into shape. They often add bacteria to create cheeses with different tastes and colors. There is a vast array of different kinds of cheeses made all over the world.

CASE STUDY

Parmesan

It takes 1,100 pounds (500 kg) of milk to make 84 pounds (38 kg) of Italian Parmesan. A cheesemaker presses the curd into a wheel shape, which is then soaked in salty water for nearly a month. The Parmesans are then stacked, and stored in large, airy storerooms for up to three years, to develop a sweet, rich flavor before they are sold.

PROCESSING MEAT AND FISH

A nimals on livestock and fish farms are reared to be killed. The dead animals, or carcasses, are processed into joints or other forms of meat and fish. They are then ready to be sold to people to cook and eat.

Meat Matters

Most livestock in rich countries are killed in slaughterhouses. It is very important to minimize distress for livestock during transportation from the farm where they lived. If animals are packed into trucks and taken long distances, they may get stressed and injured along the way. At a slaughterhouse, the livestock are usually stunned quickly with a strong electric shock or special gun before being killed. Workers use machines to help remove the hair, feathers, and other unwanted parts from the carcasses. Butchers cut up the carcasses into different parts, such as ribs, shoulder, or leg. They grind up meat to mix with other ingredients, such as seasoning for processed meat products, including burgers.

▲ *Livestock are herded together and taken to slaughterhouses to be killed. Ideally, they should not have to travel too far or become too stressed.*

Religions and Food

Some religions have special rules for how animals are killed and how meat is processed. For example, halal meat is produced according to Islamic law and kosher meat, according to Jewish law. In both halal and kosher slaughter, an animal is killed with one cut from a razor-sharp knife across the throat, and a prayer is said. Religious beliefs also affect what types of meat people eat. Neither Jewish people nor Muslims may eat pork, or any foods containing pork, and Hindus do not eat beef.

Farmed Fish

Shellfish, such as crabs and shrimp, are caught in nets and then often transported alive in water in chilled boxes to fish-processing factories or stores. Farmed fish are killed when they reach the right size for sale. Most fish are frozen before they are transported, to keep them fresh. In fish factories, workers prepare the fish to be sold. They may remove the shells from, and cook, shrimp and some other shellfish. They remove the bones, guts, and skin from fish and cut them into portions.

▲ *Salmon are reared in large numbers on fish farms. They are killed on the farm before being sent to factories for processing.*

SPOILED FOOD

A major challenge for farmers and food manufacturers is keeping food fresh and safe for customers to eat. Some foods, such as potatoes, stay fresh for months but others, including milk, only last a few days before becoming spoiled and unusable.

Attack!

Spoiled food can be discolored, mushy, slimy, smelly, and taste different from fresh food. Some food spoils because bacteria, mold (a type of fungus), and other organisms in the air attack it. These consume the food and increase in numbers. They change the chemicals in the food and alter the way it looks. For example, mold usually gives food a green, powdery surface. Another problem is that animals, such as rats and insects, may eat the food and contaminate it with bacteria from their bodies. It is especially important to always prepare food under clean, hygienic conditions, so that no dangerous bacteria, which could make us sick, get into it. Food also spoils by oxidation.

HOW LONG WILL FOOD STAY FRESH?

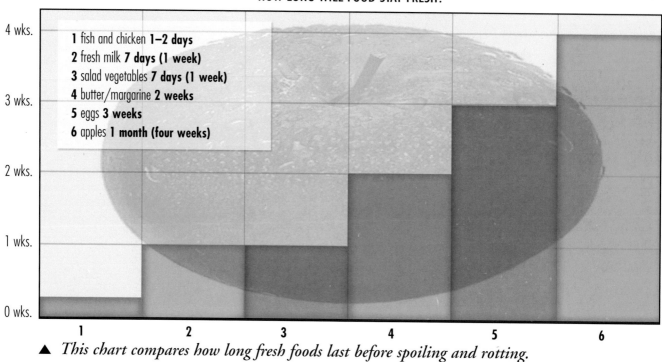

1 fish and chicken **1–2 days**
2 fresh milk **7 days (1 week)**
3 salad vegetables **7 days (1 week)**
4 butter/margarine **2 weeks**
5 eggs **3 weeks**
6 apples **1 month (four weeks)**

▲ *This chart compares how long fresh foods last before spoiling and rotting.*

▲ *It is important to store food properly to prevent it from rotting too quickly. Rotten food has to be thrown away, and this is wasteful.*

This is when oxygen in the air reacts with chemicals in the food. For example, bruised apples quickly turn brown because chemicals in the fruit oxidize. When fats, such as butter or margarine, oxidize, their taste and smell turns bad. We say they have gone rancid. To help us know how long we can keep food before it will spoil, producers often date-stamp it. They print a date on the packaging, which tells us when we should eat the food by. After that, it may start to go bad, even if it is stored properly.

Cool and Dry

Food usually spoils more quickly in warm, moist air. The simplest way to keep most foods fresh is to store them in a cool, dry place, such as a refrigerator. This slows down the growth of bacteria and mold, but does not kill them. In rich countries, people often buy more food than they can eat and so some food spoils while in storage. In the United States, it is thought that people throw away 40–50 percent of the food they buy.

FOOD DANGER

When people eat spoiled food that is full of harmful bacteria, they can suffer from food poisoning. They may vomit, have diarrhea, stomach pains, and other health problems. One of the most common bacteria that causes food poisoning is salmonella, which is sometimes found in raw chicken or eggs. It is very important to store cooked and uncooked meat separately, to avoid dangerous bacteria spreading between the two. This is called cross-contamination.

PRESERVING FOOD

There are many different ways to preserve food and stop it from spoiling. Preserved food can be stored for longer than fresh food between the time it is produced and the time it is sold and eaten.

Canning and Freezing

Foods can be preserved by canning them. Beans, for example, may be cooked, packed in salty water, and then sealed in airtight cans. This process stops bacteria in the air from getting to the food. Freezing is one of the most widely-used methods of preserving food. Most bacteria cannot feed or grow in very cold temperatures, so spoiling is extremely slow. Frozen food can remain safe to eat for many

▲ *In the food industry, most frozen foods, such as peas and fish, are preserved by flash-freezing. Machines blast food with air that is much colder than ice, so it freezes solid in a matter of minutes.*

months so long as it remains colder than 14°F (-10°C), in a freezer. Some foods are unsuitable for freezing, because the process damages them. For instance, frozen lettuces turn to mush when they are defrosted, because freezing breaks down the delicate structure of their leaves.

Drying, Smoking, and Salting

Food can be dried by using evaporation to get rid of any water in it. Without water, bacteria cannot spoil food. When it is dried, food usually shrivels up, and changes color and flavor. People dry many foods, from grains to tomatoes and grapes. Sometimes, they spread the food out in the sun, and let it dry that way. Some foods, such as fish or meat, can be dried over smoky wood fires. Hot smoke dries food fast and gives it a smoky flavor. Food can also be stored in salt. This draws the water from the food, and makes it harder.

WAXED FRUIT

Farmers sometimes spray apples, oranges, and other fruits with a thin coating of wax so they look shiny and attractive in stores. They use natural waxes, such as beeswax, that are safe to eat. Waxes also act like a waterproof layer to slow the loss of water and prevent the foods from shriveling.

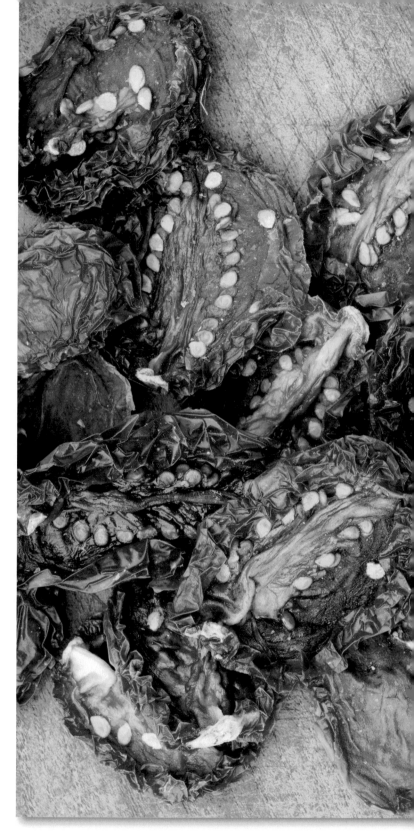

▲ *Tomatoes can be cut open and dried out in the sun. This is a traditional way of preserving many fruits in places with hot climates.*

PREPARED FOOD

In the past, people nearly always ate meals they cooked themselves from fresh or preserved ingredients. This is still true in much of the world today, especially in poor countries. But in rich countries, many people eat prepared or processed food.

Types of Prepared Food

Prepared food is cooked in factories, and only needs to be heated up before serving. People buy this kind of food because they have busy working or social lives, and have little time for making meals. Processed foods often store better than fresh foods. They are usually more consistent in taste or quality, which means the people who eat them can always be sure the foods will taste the same. However, they are more expensive and not always as nutritious as fresh food. The simplest prepared or convenience foods include fruit and vegetables that have been peeled and chopped ready for use.

▶ *A prepared meal, such as this chicken dinner, is soon ready to eat after it has been reheated in a microwave.*

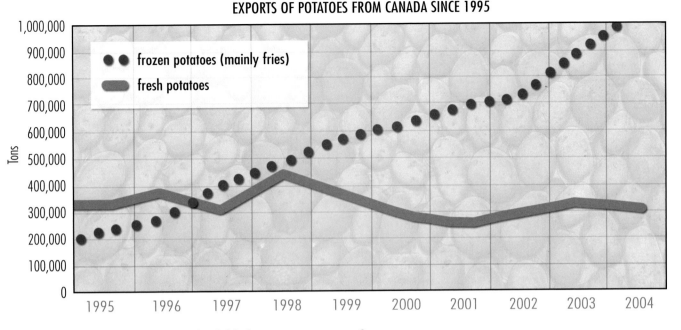

▲ *Canada is the world's fifth-largest exporter of potatoes. Over half of its potatoes are processed to become frozen products, such as french fries. The graph shows how exports of frozen potatoes (mainly fries) have overtaken fresh potato exports.*

To prepare bags of salads, workers wash lettuce in large tanks of water containing chemicals to kill insects on the leaves, and then select leaves of different types to make the right salad mix. In some food factories, workers put together more complicated dishes. These include pizzas and pies for baking, and pre-prepared meals of meat or fish with vegetables and sauces. These meals simply need to be cooked in a microwave before eating.

Food Hygiene

Workers in food factories have to take special care to avoid getting bacteria on the food they are processing. They wash and dry their hands thoroughly before work and after breaks to stop cross-contamination. They may wear hairnets, gloves, masks, and aprons to stop dirt from their bodies getting onto the food.

FOOD ALLERGIES

Many people have food allergies. This means they can get sick if they eat certain types of food. For instance, some people have severe breathing problems if they eat peanuts or anything that has even touched peanuts. In food factories where workers make a range of prepared foods, they take care to avoid contaminating food with peanuts. They may have to warn customers if there is any chance the food has been in contact with any kind of nuts.

FOOD ADDITIVES

Food additives are chemicals added to foods as they are processed. Some additives are natural, but others are made in factories. Many food additives improve the look, taste, and texture of food.

Flavorings and Colorings

There are a great number of additives used in factory-prepared foods and in some countries, these must all be listed on food packaging. Additives may be listed by their chemical names—for example, acetic acid, which is the main ingredient in vinegar and makes food taste sharp. Flavorings such as salt, sugar, sweeteners, and vanilla give foods a particular taste—they can make colas very sweet. Some flavorings improve the savory taste of foods, such as meat. One very common flavor enhancer is monosodium glutamate (MSG), which is a white powder made from sugar beet and other crops. Colorings make some foods look more attractive. For example, people add the food coloring annatto to smoked fish to give it a yellow-orange color. In some countries, bread made with white flour is colored brown, to make it look like healthier, whole-wheat bread.

▲ *Candy often contain colorings to make them look attractive, but some people are afraid these may be bad for our health.*

MORE ADDITIVES

Additives in prepared food include antioxidants, such as Vitamin C, which stop food from oxidizing and changing its color and texture. Others are anticaking agents, to make salt and other powders flow more easily without forming clumps; thickeners (often made from seaweed), to make sauces less runny, and emulsifiers, which stop foods, such as mayonnaise, from separating into oil and water. Few additives of these kinds are used in home-cooked food. Although they can make food taste fresher for longer, the additives themselves, and the fact that food may seem fresher than it really is, may result in health risks.

Additives and Safety

Food additives are generally safe to eat in small amounts, but some prepared foods contain too many of certain additives, including salt and sugar. They may also contain more fat than home-cooked food. People who eat a lot of prepared meals can develop health problems. For example, a diet high in salt can cause high blood pressure, which can lead to heart attacks. Most people agree that a diet with more fresh foods than pre-prepared meals is healthier.

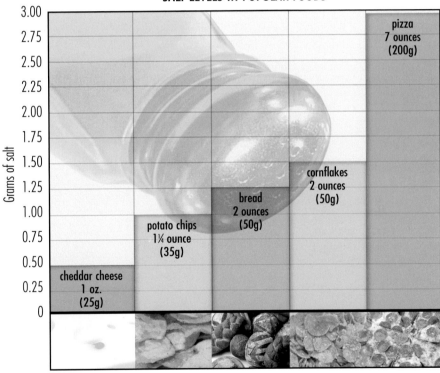

SALT LEVELS IN POPULAR FOODS

Grams of salt

- pizza 7 ounces (200g)
- cornflakes 2 ounces (50g)
- bread 2 ounces (50g)
- potato chips 1¼ ounce (35g)
- cheddar cheese 1 oz. (25g)

▲ *This chart shows how much salt there is in foods we eat every day. For example, 1 ounce (25 g) of cheddar cheese contains around half a gram of salt. Too much salt is bad for our health: 11–14 year olds should eat no more than 6 grams a day.*

PACKAGING

The food for sale in stores in rich countries is packaged in a variety of ways. Packaging stops the food from spilling, or being damaged while it is in storage or is being transported. It protects the food from contamination and spoiling, and it can carry information.

Types of Packaging

Liquids, such as juices, jellies, and sauces, are usually packed in glass or plastic bottles, cans, or waterproof, waxed cardboard cartons. Delicate foods, such as eggs, are often sold in cardboard or plastic packs that protect the food from damage. Dry powdered foods, such as sugar or flour, may be packaged in thick paper bags rather than plastic. This is so that the food can dry out quickly if moisture from the air gets into it.

◀ *Packaging can be attractive and also useful, especially if it carries information about the ingredients the food is made from, and how to store it. It also keeps food clean and fresh.*

Some people argue that we use too much packaging, especially plastic, which is hard to recycle. Plastic creates huge amounts of garbage and takes many years to decay, and so is harmful to the environment.

Design and Labeling

Packaging is often designed to make food look attractive. Consumers can also find out about what they are buying from information written on the packaging. Labels inform them what type of food is inside, the ingredients it contains, which company made or supplied the food, and sometimes, where it was grown or processed. Labels also supply nutritional information, such as the calories in a single cookie in a pack, and warnings for people with food allergies, for instance, whether the cookies contain peanuts.

▼ *Many fruits and vegetables are sold on plastic trays and wrapped in transparent plastic covers, to protect them and prevent them from drying out while on supermarket shelves. These foods could be sold in cardboard or paper packaging that does not cause environmental problems.*

CASE STUDY

Traffic Lights

In the UK, food packagers now often use a system of colored labels to show shoppers how healthy different foods are. One of the main ways this is done is using the "traffic light" nutrition label. This uses red, amber, and green colors to highlight the fat, sugar, and salt levels in food. It is unhealthy to eat too many of these. Red means the levels are high, amber medium, and green low. Consumers can tell at a glance which foods they can eat more of, and plan healthy diets.

TRANSPORTING FOOD

After food is grown, harvested, processed, and packaged, it is transported. Food is carried between regions, countries, and continents by aircraft, ships, trains, and trucks.

Food Miles

To make the journey from the farm to the customers, food is often packed in giant metal boxes called containers. Some containers have built-in refrigerators to stop food spoiling as it makes its journey. When we describe these long journeys, we often talk about "food miles," which are the distance food travels from farm to table. There is a direct link between food miles and the amount of fuel used for transportation and storage. This cost is added to the price of food. There is another, hidden, cost. When engines burn fuel to release energy for movement, they also produce carbon dioxide gas. This collects in the atmosphere and traps heat from the sun.

Scientists believe this is causing our climate to get warmer. It is referred to as "global warming."

Going Local

Many people in rich countries are choosing to eat foods produced locally, to reduce their impact on the climate. However, eating local food means people buy less from farmers in poor countries, who need exports to survive. Also, food miles do not tell the full story about climate impact. For example, in the winter, tomatoes grown in Spain and transported to northern Europe have less impact than tomatoes grown in cold countries, where farmers rely heavily on fuel to heat greenhouses.

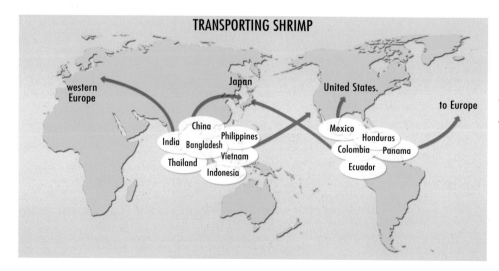

TRANSPORTING SHRIMP

western Europe

Japan

United States.

to Europe

China
India Bangladesh Philippines
Thailand Vietnam
Indonesia

Mexico
Honduras
Colombia Panama
Ecuador

◀ *Ninety percent of all farmed shrimp exported from poor countries in Asia and Central America is sent abroad and eaten by people in the rich countries of Japan, the United States, and Europe.*

▲ *Here, food is being loaded onto a ship. It will travel a long distance, but the amount of carbon dioxide emitted by the ship's engine will be less than by alternative forms of transportation.*

DEBATE

How Can We Cut Down on Food Miles?

In the United States, most people live within less than 62 miles (100 km) of an apple orchard, but the apples in typical supermarkets have traveled around 1,715 miles (2,760 km) from the farm to their table. Look at the labels on the food you eat during a day or a week. Use maps to figure out the total food miles the food traveled to get to you. If we want to cut down on food miles, is there any way we can do this and continue eating the same foods that we have always done? Or must we choose different ones?

WHAT'S FOR DINNER?

The last stage in the journey from farm to table is a store or restaurant. Most people in rich countries buy almost all of the food they consume from large supermarkets, or from smaller, specialty shops.

Buying Power

Many people grow their own food. This is common in poor countries, but even in rich countries, there are people who prefer to grow their own vegetables in their gardens or on plots, or buy locally grown food from farmers' markets or even direct from the farm. However, most food in rich countries is bought from supermarket chains. These source food from the global market, which means they have great power over the food industry. Food suppliers (farmers and processors) sell

▲ *Farmers' markets give producers the chance to sell their produce directly to customers, cutting out the distributor and supermarkets. Markets nearly always operated like this in the past—and still do in much of the world.*

food to large supermarkets at very low prices, because supermarkets buy large quantities of their produce, and can demand that farmers sell it to them at a low price. Suppliers agree to this because they do not want to risk losing such large orders.

Food Choices

The choices people make about what they buy often depend on what they think is important as well as price and quality. For example, they may prefer to buy sustainably produced food. This means the food has been produced using methods that protect and sustain farmland and other resources. It includes organic food, local food with few food miles, and fair trade food. Fair trade food guarantees a fair price and good working conditions for farmers in poor countries who depend on sales in rich countries. Consumers and producers of food are interdependent, and as a result, consumers' choices influence the range of foods the food industry produces, and the livelihoods of the producers.

ORGANIC FOOD

Organic food is farmed without artificial chemicals, such as fertilizers and weed killers. It is processed with as few food additives as possible. Organic foods are often more expensive than nonorganic foods because more labor is needed to produce them, and there is only a small amount of organic food entering the food industry. However, organic food is becoming increasingly popular.

▶ *Although many people buy processed food, fresh food is usually better for us, and tastes better, too.*

GLOSSARY

additives substances added to food. Some are complex chemicals that have only been developed in recent years, but others, such as salt, have been in use for centuries.

allergy sensitivity to certain substances, so that coming into contact with them or (with food) eating them makes the allergic person sick.

annatto a kind of red dye made from a tropical tree found in Central and South America. It is used in many kinds of foods, including cheese and butter.

antioxidants substances that stop food starting to decay or change once it has been in contact with oxygen in the air.

bacteria (singular: **bacterium**) very tiny organisms. Some do useful things, such as change milk into yogurt, but some cause disease.

blood pressure the pressure our blood exerts against the inner walls of our blood vessels as it flows through them.

carbohydrate a substance made by plants, and which is an important type of food that gives us energy.

carcass the dead body of an animal, such as a cow or a sheep. The word is not often used for other animals, such as fish.

concentrate to make a solution stronger. Juice is concentrated by removing some of the water from it.

consistent to be the same on every occasion and in every place. Foods that are consistent can always be relied upon to taste the same wherever and whenever they are bought.

contaminate make dirty or to introduce germs, making food dangerous to eat.

dairy products any foods made from milk. These include cheese, butter, yogurt, cream, and ice cream.

date-stamp mark to show the latest date by which the producer believes the food will remain fresh. It often says "Best before" and then gives a date.

emulsifiers substances that emulsify oils, which means mixing them with another kind of liquid to form a creamy substance.

evaporate to let the liquid in a substance change to a vapor or gas.

flash-freezing freezing food very quickly using very low temperatures, so that any water in them turns to ice almost at once. It is one of the best ways of preserving fresh food.

fungus (plural: **fungi**) organism similar to a plant, that lives on dead or living organic matter. Molds are fungi and so are mushrooms.

global market the countries throughout the world that trade with each other.

grain seeds, such as those produced by wheat and corn plants. Grain is often ground finely to make flour.

halal food allowed under Muslim law. Meat is only halal if the animal has been killed in a special way. Some kinds of food, such as pork, are never halal. Food that is not allowed is called haram.

heart attack a sudden failure of the heart to work properly, often causing death.

interdependent when things depend on each other to survive or make a living.

kosher food allowed under Jewish law. Some foods, such as pork, or meat cooked with milk, can never be kosher. There are special shops, or sometimes special aisles in supermarkets, where Jewish people can buy food they know is kosher.

monosodium glutamate (MSG) a chemical made from certain plants that is used in some kinds of processed food.

mold a type of fungus that forms a woolly or furry covering on substances—including food.

nutritious valuable and health-giving as a food.

organic food that has been grown in as natural a way as possible, without the use of artificial chemical fertilizers or weed killers. Many people claim it is better for us and the environment.

organism a living thing.

oxidation being changed by a chemical reaction with the oxygen in the air.

pasteurized to heat a liquid to kill harmful bacteria. Milk is pasteurized by heating it to 145°F (63°C), and then cooling it. Other liquids, such as orange juice, may also be pasteurized.

preserve any way of treating food to make it stay safe to eat for longer.

rancid sour or unpleasant-tasting.

rennet a substance used to make milk curdle and form cheese. Rennet was traditionally made from a substance taken from calves' stomachs. Today, there are vegetarian forms made from fungi.

seasoning something that makes food taste better, such as salt, pepper, or herbs.

staple foods the main energy-giving food people eat. They include rice, corn, wheat and wheat products, such as bread, and root vegetables, such as potatoes.

subsistence farms very small farms or plots where farmers grow a few crops or keep a very few animals just to feed themselves and their immediate families. In poor countries, subsistence farming may provide all the food a family gets.

sustain, sustainable to look after the land and not to damage it or produce large amounts of waste that cannot be recycled.

tropics the warmer parts of the world, close to the equator.

TOPIC WEB, FIND OUT MORE, AND WEB SITES

FROM FARM TO TABLE

Science and Environment
• Compare the rates of decay of several pieces of similar fruit. Put one in an airtight container, another in a refrigerator, another in a freezer, and another in a dark cupboard or plastic bag.
• Find out about yeasts and their importance to the food industry.
• Obesity is often linked with eating too much processed food. What are the effects of obesity on health?

English and Literacy
• Review television commercials for foods, especially those aimed at young people. These are often shown after school. Try to assess whether or not they encourage healthy eating.
• Write an article for a newspaper expressing your concerns about increasing food miles. Choose some examples that you feel make your point clearly, and suggest how we could cut back on food miles.

Geography
• Produce a flow chart of the processes in growing, picking, packing, transporting, and storing bananas from farm to table.
• Research large supermarket chains and find one that has stores in many different countries. How might their presence affect the sales of local foods?

History and Economics
• Find out about what food was available during World War II and the importance of transporting food across the Atlantic to Great Britain. An example is wheat from Canada.
• Find out about important events in farming in the past. These could include the opening up of the American West for cattle farming, the Agricultural Revolution in Great Britain, or the introduction of agriculture in Australia. How did new forms of technology help affect these events?

Art and Culture
• Design a package for a convenience meal or sandwich of your choice that does not contain any harmful additives. Include a picture that carries a message about healthy eating.
• Find out about eating insects in different world cultures, such as among the Aborigines in Australia.
• Collect songs and poems about different kinds of foods and drinks. What do the oldest ones tell us about food in the past?

FIND OUT MORE

Books

21st Century Issues: World Hunger
by Steven Maddocks (Gareth Stevens Publishing, 2004)

Food Science
by Jeanne Miller (Lerner Publications, 2008)

Sustainable World: Food and Farming
by Rob Bowden (Kidshaven Press, 2003)

Web Sites

Due to the changing nature of Internet links, PowerKids Press has developed an online list of Web sites related to the subject of this book. This site is updated regularly. Please use this link to access this list:
http://www.powerkidslinks.com/faf/table

INDEX